YOUR KNOWLEDGE HAS VALUE

Anna Jung

Critical Evaluation of the Article "Managing Talent across National Borders: The Challenges Faced by an International Retail Group" by Mehdi Boussebaa and Glenn Morgan

GRIN Verlag

Bibliografische Information der Deutschen Nationalbibliothek:

Die Deutsche Bibliothek verzeichnet diese Publikation in der Deutschen National-
bibliografie; detaillierte bibliografische Daten sind im Internet über http://dnb.d-
nb.de/ abrufbar.

Imprint:

Copyright © 2014 GRIN Verlag GmbH
Druck und Bindung: Books on Demand GmbH, Norderstedt Germany
ISBN: 978-3-656-68519-7

This book at GRIN:

http://www.grin.com/en/e-book/275396/critical-evaluation-of-the-article-managing-
talent-across-national-borders

GRIN - Your knowledge has value

Der GRIN Verlag publiziert seit 1998 wissenschaftliche Arbeiten von Studenten, Hochschullehrern und anderen Akademikern als eBook und gedrucktes Buch. Die Verlagswebsite www.grin.com ist die ideale Plattform zur Veröffentlichung von Hausarbeiten, Abschlussarbeiten, wissenschaftlichen Aufsätzen, Dissertationen und Fachbüchern.

Visit us on the internet:

http://www.grin.com/

http://www.facebook.com/grincom

http://www.twitter.com/grin_com

Managing across
Cultures

Word Count: 2747

Critical Evaluation of the Article "Managing Talent
across National Borders: The Challenges Faced by
an International Retail Group"
by Mehdi Boussebaa and Glenn Morgan

Introduction

Increasing globalisation offers a wide range of opportunities for businesses operating in an international market, and managers are required more than ever before to work with individuals from different countries (Sparrow et al., 2004). However, in order to manage effectively across national borders and to prevent misunderstandings or conflicts, it is imperative for international managers to understand the complex differences between countries and their implications for business. Against this background, it is particularly worthwhile to scrutinise existing research concerned with the current challenges faced by multinational corporations (MNCs) more closely. Accordingly, the aim of the present essay is to critically evaluate the research paper "Managing talent across national borders: the challenges faced by an international retail group" by Mehdi Boussebaa and Glenn Morgan (2008) and to provide implications for theory and practice in cross-cultural management.

First of all, to set the stage for the article analysis, a brief overview of the paper will be provided. Subsequently, theoretical frameworks used in the article will be presented and evaluated. This is followed by a critical evaluation of the appropriateness of the chosen study design and methodology for the research questions posed by the authors. Further, the findings and conclusions of the undertaken study will be outlined and discussed, and afterwards, based on the critical analysis of the paper in the previous sections, the implications for individuals involved in cross-cultural management will be presented. Finally, the essay will conclude that the reviewed research paper, despite some flaws, is an interesting piece of work that makes a contribution to the existing research on international management.

Research Paper Introduction

The research paper deals with the influences of national institutional environments on a MNC's attempt to develop a transnational talent management (TM) framework. More precisely, Boussebaa and Morgan examined in their single case study of a British-French retail group, the perceptions of British and French managers towards to the TM programme which was sought to be established by the MNC's headquarters, i.e. the UK-firm. The aim was to provide a common TM system across the British and the recently acquired French company in order to ensure consistency concerning the management of talent between the two firms. However, it should be noted that this TM framework was essentially based on the British approach to TM.

1

Based on the results of interviews with British and French managers, observation and documents, the authors have revealed considerable differences in the conception of talent management between the two companies. According to Boussebaa and Morgan, the reason for this is that the British managers held the belief that talent should be identified by measurements, such as assessment centres, whereas the French managers did not share this view as they thought they had already proven their abilities through highly competitive studies at the *grandes e'coles*. Since the corporate headquarters ignored this differing understanding of talent and thus encountered strong resistance from its subsidiary regarding the proposed TM framework, the project resulted in a complete failure. Based on these findings, the authors point to the major difficulties associated with implementing transnational management practices which can be attributed to the prevailing institutional differences between nations.

Theory and Literature

In order to underline the significance of their findings, Boussebaa and Morgan draw firstly upon mainstream international management literature that essentially maintains that national differences are no longer significant to the management and organisation of MNCs. In this context, the authors particularly refer to Perlmutter (1969) and Bartlett and Ghoshal (1989) who supported this thesis of convergence in management practices and argued that MNCs would evolve over time to respectively geocentric and transnational companies. However, the authors strongly challenge this view and refer in this regard to the increasing research drawing upon comparative institutionalism. Further, they provide various research evidence for the persistence of national differences and point to an existing dialectical relationship marked by micro-political bargaining between headquarters and subsidiaries. Moreover, Boussebaa and Morgan provide, based on a comparative analysis, detailed and significant background information concerning the development and promotion of managers in the investigated countries.

All in all, the theoretical underpinning employed by the authors seems to be appropriate for the conducted study. First, the authors highlight the predominant assumptions in the mainstream international management literature regarding the decreased relevance of national differences to the management of MNCs and subsequently they provide the latest counter evidence for this thesis from various comparative institutionalist research. However, although Perlmutter is one of the earliest and most significant international management theorists, it would have reinforced the authors' position if they had provided additional and more recent research underpinning this allegedly still prevailing convergence thesis. Further, the literature used for the comparison of French and British management development and promotion processes is mainly from the 1980s/1990s and accordingly not up to date. More recent sources would have been beneficial at this stage.

However, more importantly, given the fact that the paper deals with differences across countries and their impact on international business management, it is surprising that the authors did not refer to classical cross-cultural communication theorists such as Hofstede or Trompenaars. Although, for example, Hofstede's framework of national cultural values (1984) is too simplistic as it ignores the diverse and complex nature of cultures (Alcadipani Da Silveira & Crubelatte, 2007; McSweeny, 2002; Patel, 2014), it would still have been useful to discuss its relevance in the context of the differing perceptions of management across national borders.

Research Approach

In contrast to previous research, the authors adopted a comparative institutionalist approach rather than that of mainstream international management. Further, the paper is based on an empirical qualitative case study of a British-French group, which was conducted over two weeks in 2003, and on the analysis of secondary data in the form of internal and external documents such as annual reports or documents related to the TM framework. More precisely, Boussebaa and Morgan conducted 13 semi-structured interviews with line managers and HR staff in the French as well as in the British company. Additionally, they collected data during informal conversations and recorded direct observations during meetings and workshops.

Both the chosen research design and the research methods appear to be suitable for the research questions posed by the authors. Since the aim of the study was to explore the influence of national institutional contexts, a qualitative field research approach was an appropriate method for this purpose as it enabled to gather an in-depth understanding of the managerial experiences and perceptions of the TM framework. Particularly, direct observation during a training course was a useful technique which facilitated observing more subtle communications (Babbie, 2007; Bryman & Bell, 2011) between managers and thus contributed to the understanding of their attitudes towards the concept of TM. Finally, the analysis of collected documents complemented the primary research by providing additional information concerning the organisational background and the TM system.

However, one important limitation of the research approach, recognised by the researchers themselves, is the lack of generalisation potential of the findings due to the use of only one case study (Yin, 2009). This is particularly noteworthy given that this case deals with an uncommon headquarters-subsidiary relationship as the subsidiary is of similar size and hence strength to that of the headquarters. Moreover, the authors could have provided a more detailed justification for the chosen research methodology to underline its appropriateness for the study.

Researchers' Findings and Conclusions

Boussebaa and Morgan revealed in their study that the striking differences between French and British institutional frameworks for education and development had a great impact on the managers' attitudes towards the concept of TM. According to the study, the French managers were highly resistant to the proposed establishment of the UK-instituted TM programme as they believed that they had already proven their talent by the obtainment of *grandes e'coles* diplomas. The British company, however, did not take this differing understanding of TM into account and considered its approach to TM to be readily transferable to its subsidiary in France. In other words, by ignoring these differences, the British headquarters contributed significantly to the ultimate failure of the project. Based on these findings, the authors point to continued national differences and conclude that a high degree of 'institutional distance' between companies tend to result in difficulties in implementing transnational management systems.

Generally speaking, the findings and conclusions derived from the study seem to be reasonable and justified. The statements from the interviews as well as the observation demonstrated significant differences in attitudes between the French and British managers towards the management of talent which were influenced by institutional contexts in the respective countries. In this way, Boussebaa and Morgan have refuted the thesis of converging management practices which is largely supported by international management theorists. Their argument is further reinforced by a recent study by one of the authors which has revealed persistent cross-national differences in the area of management consultancy (Taminiau et al., 2012). Further, Kim and McLean (2012) suggest in a similar way to the

4

paper that an ethnocentric approach, which was essentially taken by the MNC headquarters, presents one of the main challenges in developing global talent.

Nevertheless, the specific circumstances of the investigated case study have to be considered. Given the fact that the two firms were of comparable size and hence the taking over of the French company was associated with substantial tensions, it can be assumed that the resistant behaviour by the subsidiary was likely to emerge. However, research indicates that even if subsidiaries do not have a similarly strong power position as that of their headquarters, local managers are able to engage with micro-political negotiating processes (Dörrenbächer & Gammelgaard, 2006).

Furthermore, it seems that Boussebaa and Morgan tend to generalise their findings, and, similar to Hofstede, classify British managers, for example, as practice-oriented, and French managers, on the other hand, as classified by their academic achievements in regard to their career opportunities. Accordingly, the authors do not refer to potential perceptions differences regarding the development of talent that might exist among French or British managers.

Implications for Individuals Involved in Cross-Cultural Management
Drawing upon the analysis of the paper, important implications for both research and practice in cross-cultural management can be derived. In essence, the article highlights the significant impact of institutional environments on individuals' attitudes towards management practices such as the development of talent. For this reason, more comparative institutional research between other countries is necessary in order to extend this single case study. However, although the institutional influences are important and have to be considered accordingly, the cultural aspects should not be ignored. Therefore, researchers should seek to take into account the institutional as well as the cultural factors when investigating management across borders. Additionally, the wider organisational context has to be considered in order to reduce potential biases in the analysis of the research findings.

Furthermore, the paper provides equally important implications for individuals working in a cross-cultural environment. First of all, particularly headquarters managers have to become aware that differences between their and the subsidiary managers' perceptions towards management practices might exist. However, creating this awareness is fundamental but not sufficient for a successful headquarters-subsidiary relationship. Further, it is vital to understand the underlying assumptions behind these differences. As Boussebaa and Morgan suggest, differing institutional environments across boundaries present an explanation for the major difficulties associated with the introduction of corporate-wide standards. However, according to various researchers such as Hofstede (1984) and Trompenaars (2011), 'cultural distance' is a significant, if not the most important, reason for conflicts in international business. Although, Hofstede's work in particular is widely accepted, it is of paramount importance to consider the plurality and heterogeneity within countries and organisations (Alcadipani Da Silveira & Crubelatte, 2007; McSweeny, 2002), which are entirely ignored by his model. Similarly, supporting this critique, Chapman et al. (2008) provide evidence that 'small cultural distance' can cause more tensions than 'large cultural distance' and highlight in this way the importance of *perceived* rather than that of *absolute* cultural distance, which is proposed by Hofstede (1984).

Additionally, based on the findings from the paper, it is important to point out that international managers should avoid taking an ethnocentric approach and assuming the transferability of organisational practices across borders (Schneider, 2003). Rather, they should question and reflect on their own practice and be willing to deal with potential problems associated with cross-cultural management. Development of skills such as culture intelligence (Earley & Mosakowski, 2004; Livermore, 2010) and the ability to take different viewpoints are of great importance in order to minimise conflicts and misunderstandings and thus be able to benefit from the various advantages associated with multicultural working (Stahl et al., 2010).

Conclusion

Drawing upon the critical evaluation of the paper in this essay, it can be concluded that, despite some flaws, the article presents an important contribution to the research, particularly in the hardly explored field of global TM. The institutionalist approach adopted by the researchers offers an alternative perspective to potential causes of tensions in MNCs and provides counter evidence for the allegedly predominant transnational and geocentric orientation of MNCs. Further, this essay has illustrated the highly complex nature of cross-cultural management and pointed to the significant importance of developing an understanding of different cultures to succeed in international business.

Reflective Account

'Managing across cultures' was not only a very interesting and partly very eye-opening module, but also highly useful for my future career in, hopefully, a multinational company. Although I grew up in two different countries (Ukraine, Germany), and have gained during my internship in India extremely valuable experience in living and working in an entirely different culture compared to my own, studying with students from all over the world developed my understanding of other cultures to a great extent.

The group work in particular, highlighted the difficulties arising from multinational working and demonstrated the vital importance of developing a cultural awareness in order to benefit from the various advantages associated with multicultural teams (Stahl et al., 2010). It was indeed a bit challenging for me to work with my group members as I noticed that we had not the same expectations regarding the quality of the outcome of our group work. This can certainly be partly explained by different educational backgrounds. In other words, as Boussebaa and Morgan (2008) revealed in their study, institutional contexts make an impact on our perceptions and attitudes. Furthermore, Germany is often associated with diligence and precision in work. China, on the other hand, tends to place not the same emphasis on perfection and accuracy in working. However, my experience confirmed that these 'stereotypes' cannot be generalised and applied to every German/Chinese. Other factors such as personality or upbringing play a critical role in this context and decisively affect our behaviour.

One example that demonstrates the challenges in multinational teams is the different perception of time (Hall, 1959). Again, Germans are known for their punctuality. Asian and African countries, for instance, do not attach the same importance to it. Since I anticipated this potential issue due to my previous experience in working with Chinese/African students, I always finished my E-mails to the group members with the sentence: "Please be on time, British time ;-)". In the end, partly because we knew we had to work efficiently due to other coursework pressure, everything went quite well.

Further differences became obvious in regard to participation style and amount. But again, although culture plays a significant role in this context, other factors such as age, experience and the importance attached to the studies influence our attitude towards the willingness to participate. However, language as a significant communication and participation barrier has also to be considered. It is clear that if someone has difficulties to understand the article, he/she will probably not be able to contribute greatly to the discussion. Further, even if the person would like to participate, he/she might feel inhibited by the language problems he/she is facing. It appears to be common sense to make these conclusions but I noticed that personally I have become more aware of these strong interrelations between language level, motivation and willingness to participate through writing this reflection report.

Through this module I have become even more aware of how important it is for effective cross-cultural working to be able to take different viewpoints and to reflect continuously on personal behaviour and judgement towards individuals from a different cultural background. This is particularly vital since we are often not aware that we are inclined to stereotyping and tend to be ethnocentric orientated towards other cultures.

References:

Alcadipani Da Silveira, R. & Crubelatte, J. (2007) 'The Notion of Brazilian Organizational Culture Questionable Generalizations and Vague Concepts. *Critical Perspectives on International Business.* 3(2). pp. 150-169.

Babbie, E. (2007) *The Basics of Social Research.* 4rd edn. Belmont: Thomson Wadsworth.

Boussebaa, M. & Morgan, G. (2008) 'Managing Talent across National Borders: The Challenges Faced by an International Retail Group'. *Critical Perspectives on International Business.* 4(1). pp. 25-41.

Bryman, A. & Bell, E. (2011) *Business Research Methods.* 3rd edn. Oxford: Oxford University Press.

Chapman, M., Gajewska-De Mattos, H., Clegg, J. & Buckley, P. J. (2008) 'Close Neighbours and Distant Friends - Perceptions of Cultural Distance'. *International Business Review.* 17(3). pp. 217-234.

Earley, P. C. & Mosakowski, E. (2004) 'Cultural Intelligence'. *Harvard Business Review.* 82(10). pp. 139-146.

Hall, E. T. (1959) *The Silent Language.* New York: Anchor Books Doubleday. [Online] Available at: http://globalsociology.ucoz.ru/_ld/0/3_SilentLanguage0.pdf [Accessed: 06 April, 2014].

Hofstede, G. (1984) *Culture's Consequences: International Differences in Work-Related Values.* Abridged edn. Newbury Park: Sage.

Dörrenbächer, C. & Gammelgaard, J. (2006) 'Subsidiary Role Development: The Effect of Micro-Political Headquarters–Subsidiary Negotiations on the Product, Market and Value-Added Scope of Foreign-Owned Subsidiaries.' *Journal of International Management.* 12(3). pp. 266-283.

Kim, S. & McLean, G. N. (2012) 'Global Talent Management: Necessity, Challenges, and the Roles of HRD'. *Advances in Developing Human Resources.* 14(4). pp. 566-585.

Livermore, D. (2010) *Leading with Cultural Intelligence: The New Secret to Success.* New York: Amacon.

McSweeny, B. (2002) 'Hofstede's Model of National Cultural Differences and Their Consequences: A Triumph of Faith – a Failure of Analysis'. *Human Relations.* 55(1). pp.89-118.

Patel, T. (2014) *Cross-Cultural Management: A Transnational Approach.* London: Routledge.

Schneider, S. C. & Barsoux, J. (2003) *Managing across Cultures.* 2nd edn. London: Prentice Hall.

Stahl, G. K., Maznevski, M. L., Voigt, A. Jonsen, K. (2010) 'Unraveling the Effects of Cultural Diversity in Teams: A Meta-Analysis of Research on Multicultural Work Groups'. *Journal of International Business Studies.* 41(4). pp. 690-709.

Sparrow, P., Brewster, C. & Harris, H. (2004) *Globalizing Human Resource Management.* London/New York: Routledge.

Taminiaua, Y., Boussebaa, M. & Berghmana, L. (2012) 'Convergence or Divergence? A Comparison of Informal Consultant–Client Relationship Development Practices in Britain, France and Germany'. *The Service Industries Journal.* 32(10). pp. 1707–1720.

Trompenaars, F. & Hampden-Turner, C. (2011) *Riding the Waves of Culture: Understanding Diversity in Global Business.* London: Nicholas Brealey.

Yin, R. K. (2009) *Case Study Research: Design and Methods.* 4th edn. London: Sage.